BOOK ANALYSIS

Written by Baptiste Frankinet
Translated by Carly Probert

AF143893

Bel Ami

BY GUY DE MAUPASSANT

GUY DE MAUPASSANT 1

French novelist and short-story writer

BEL AMI 2

A picture of society

SUMMARY 3

Part one – from a mediocre life to a comfortable situation

Part two – achieving social recognition

CHARACTER STUDY 8

Male characters

Female characters

ANALYSIS 13

Women and love

 A satire of the press

A novel between realism and naturalism

Autobiographical elements

FURTHER REFLECTION 19

Some questions to think about...

FURTHER READING 21

GUY DE MAUPASSANT

FRENCH NOVELIST AND SHORT-STORY WRITER

- **Born in Tourville-sur-Arques in 1850**
- **Died in Paris in 1893**
- **Notable works:**
  - *Boule de suif* (1880), short story
  - *Contes de la Bécasse* (1883), short story collection
  - *Bel Ami* (1885), novel

Born in 1850, Guy de Maupassant was a French writer who produced a total of six novels and over three hundred short stories. He spent his childhood in Normandy, where he began studies in law. In 1870, he enlisted as a volunteer in the Franco-Prussian War, before moving to Paris where he worked as a civil servant. Gustave Flaubert, a friend of his mother, took him under his wing and introduced him to the literary circles. He mixed with the realist and naturalist writers of his time, including Émile Zola. From 1880 to 1890, he wrote novels (*Une Vie, Bel Ami*) and many realist short stories (*Boule de suif, La Maison Tellier*, etc.) and fantastic short stories (*The Horla, Fear*, etc.) in which he presents his pessimistic vision of society. He sank into insanity in 1890 and died in 1893.

BEL AMI

A PICTURE OF SOCIETY

- **Genre:** realist novel
- **Reference edition:** De Maupassant, G. (Unknown) *Bel-Ami*. Lausanne: Éditions Rencontre.
- **First edition:** 1885
- **Themes:** women, love, professional field, social ascension, colonialism

A realist novel published in 1885, *Bel Ami* recounts the social ascension of a provincial man arriving in Paris, Georges Duroy. Maupassant used his story to portray the society in which he lived and to criticize colonial politics and the influence of women on the professional world, especially the world of the press. Through his hero, the author shares his own experience and, at times, Georges Duroy passes as a literary transposition of Maupassant.

Many directors and screenwriters have been captivated by the realism of the story and have contributed, with their adaptations, to the intergenerational success of the novel.

SUMMARY

Georges Duroy, a former soldier living in Paris, is driven by an insatiable desire to succeed in the world. Luck leads him to meet a former regimental comrade, Charles Forestier. Charles has achieved great social success, since he is the political editor of *La Vie Française*. He strongly advises his friend to follow his own path and offers him a boost: an invitation to a dinner at his home.

This dinner brings together Monsieur and Madame Forestier, Madame de Marelle, a friend of the couple, and her daughter, as well as Monsieur Walter, the owner and chief editor of *La Vie Française*, and his wife. The three women constantly admire Duroy's spirit, and Monsieur Walter offers to take him on as a clerk and editor of a small column in which he will recount his memories of the war. But soon, Duroy realizes how little he knows about this type of exercise, which he has never done before. He then asks for the help of his friend Forestier who puts him into the hands of his wife, who is an expert in the art of writing articles herself. The next day, Duroy discovers the joy of reading his own article. Little by little, he familiarizes himself with the daily work on the newspaper, but he does not progress in the art of writing and is forced to abandon his column.

On the advice of Madame Forestier, Duroy regularly visits Madame de Marelle. Soon, he begins to court her, although she is married. She succumbs to the one she calls Bel Ami and becomes his mistress. However, Duroy is now forced to lead a grander lifestyle than he can afford. His debts and loans multiply, and he is obliged to accept, with a heavy heart, financial gifts from Madame de Marelle, who is much richer than he is. One day, however, she learns that he is continuing to court other women and decides to leave him immediately.

Duroy then takes the opportunity to court Madame Forestier. She pushes him away and advises him to visit Madame Walter. He follows her advice and shows off his flair and wickedness before a group of guests present there. The next day, he is entrusted with a more important job position, with better pay, and is invited to all of the dinners organized by the Walter family. From then on, Duroy is at the same social level as Forestier. Meanwhile, the latter suffers from a cough that forces him to leave Paris and go to Cannes.

The position of social editor which Duroy acquired thanks to his powers of seduction earns him enemies as well as friends. He is harshly criticized by an anonymous writer in a competitor newspaper. Discovering the identity of this critic, he challenges him to a duel. Luckily, the guns used in this altercation do not injure either of the enemies. Duroy comes out of it with an even greater aura, which strengthens and improves his position in the newspaper even more.

In the days that follow, Madeleine Forestier writes to Bel Ami to tell him that her husband's days are numbered. Duroy then rushes to his friend's bedside and stays with him until his death a few days later. On the day of the burial, he plucks up the courage and confesses his love to Madeleine for a second time. She asks him to be patient.

PART TWO – ACHIEVING SOCIAL RECOGNITION

Madeleine marries Bel Ami, but not without encouraging him to impersonate a provincial nobleman: Du Roy de Cantel. She also insists that they visit her husband's parents. However, a huge gap lies between Madeleine and Duroy's family. This divide is the first problem, and others soon follow: Bel Ami replaces Forestier in his duties and the comparison between them becomes difficult to bear. In addition, those around the Forestier couple – Comte de Vaudrec, Laroche-Mathieu, etc. – show up at the couple's house as if nothing had changed.

For these reasons, and particularly as Madeleine remains silent in front of his troubles, Duroy turns away from his wife and resumes his meetings with Madame de Marelle. Moreover, he seduces Madame Walter. Madame Walter gives in, but not without remorse.

At the newspaper, a press campaign organized by Madeleine Duroy brings the demise of the Ministry of Foreign Affairs. Thanks to this, Laroche-Mathieu becomes minister and the newspaper thus becomes the main communication tool of the Ministry. Henceforth, *La Vie Française* is no longer a second-class newspaper, but a reference point in the world of the press. Bel Ami takes advantage of this to resume his column.

However, the minister deliberately deceives Duroy for his own interests. He suggests in the press that France has lost interest in Morocco and leaves Spain to gain a stranglehold there. Yet, shortly after, he orders the military to invade Morocco. Now, since public opinion was unaware of the event, Moroccan lending rates have not increased. For their part, Laroche-Mathieu and a few others have profited from this by buying cheap shares in this loan, before they are redeemed by France at a higher price. The minister, Walter and others, sharing this insider knowledge, get rich off the back of Duroy. Madame Walter, in love with Bel Ami, reveals what is happening and suggests that he also buys a share of the loan. He agrees, but he is already disappointed with the vapid relationship he has with his boss' wife. He unashamedly abandons her.

Soon after, Comte de Vaudrec, a dear friend of Madeleine, becomes very ill. He will die and bequeath his entire fortune to his friend. Annoyed because he is excluded from the will, Duroy claims half of the inheritance so as not to have to endure the shame of being a cuckolded husband. Duroy and Madeleine are now in possession of a fortune worth several million.

However, this is not enough for Bel Ami. His boss has earned nearly 50 million from the Morocco affair and has become one of the masters of the world. Madame Walter is trying as much as she can to have Bel Ami benefit from it, but he ostensibly detaches himself from her. Only Suzanne, the youngest daughter of the Walters, interests him. During a fashionable dinner organized in the Walters' new home, Bel Ami notices Laroche-Mathieu's attachment to Madeleine. He decides to take advantage of the indelicate situation he has been put in by his unfaithful wife.

A few days later, Duroy catches Laroche-Mathieu and Madeleine committing adultery. This revelation leads him to seek a divorce. The press gets hold of the affair and brings down the minister. The newspaper, far from wanting to be buried along with him, prefers to denounce him and come back stronger.

The months that follow ensure the total success of Duroy: he manages to convince Suzanne to marry him and, in order to get the young woman's parents to agree to the marriage, he kidnaps her. Cornered, Walter gives his consent, even though his wife is trapped in a kind of madness at seeing her former lover become her daughter's husband.

The consecration of Bel Ami's career comes at the same time as his marriage. The church of Madeleine is packed for their wedding, as if they were royalty. This is the apotheosis of his ascension.

CHARACTER STUDY

Georges Duroy/Bel Ami

Georges Duroy initially appears as a common character. However, his personality is marked by an incredible ambition: he wants to be rich and powerful and become one who surpasses everyone with his success.

Throughout the novel, the hero follows a progressive course. With the exception of the first stage, which he manages with the help of Forestier, each step of his ascent is accomplished through the intervention of a woman: Madeleine, Madame Walter, then Suzanne Walter. Curiously, Bel Ami can rely on the charm that he exerts over women. But these victories alone, which are too easily conquered, cannot lead to his success. Duroy is intelligent enough not to seek too much status too fast. While his career is taking off, he takes the time to master every task he is entrusted with. He becomes a professional writer, his flair is made increasingly sharp and his character gradually hardens. His success is therefore also due to his knowledge of the social, moral and political milieu in which he moves. He is very much an opportunist.

Some have noted the resemblance of Maupassant to the character of Georges Duroy. It is true that the similarities are occasionally significant: the same physical appearance, the same path, the same determination to succeed. Perhaps Maupassant was in fact telling his own story through that of his hero.

Charles Forestier

In the first chapters, Forestier represents someone who has succeeded: he has an excellent job, a beautiful wife and leads a worldly life. For Duroy, he represents a role model to follow, a quiet strength for whom success comes easy.

However, Forestier is not as strong a character as Bel Ami. The reader discovers that he has many limitations: he is a puppet manipulated by his wife, to whom he owes all of his success; he suffers from poor health; the fear of death tortures him, even in his final moments.

Throughout the story, Forestier no longer assumes the position of a role model, but becomes the equal of Duroy. After his death, when Duroy takes his place in his household, Forestier becomes a hated man who has been surpassed and devalued.

Laroche-Mathieu

An inconsistent politician, Laroche-Mathieu is guided by nothing but greed. Basically, Laroche-Mathieu is not the guarantor of his own success; he succeeds thanks to the contributions of others: Walter turns him into his alter ego in politics and Madeleine organizes his promotion campaign. Unfortunately for him, he is unable to avoid the pitfalls and fails when faced with a stronger force. He does not survive the scandal caused by the confession of adultery.

Monsieur Walter

Rich, thirsty for power and easy money, Monsieur Walter

created the newspaper to support his shares on the stock market and does not try to make it a recognised media organization. However, while he takes advantage of everyone, he forces Duroy to defend his honor at the risk of his life. He is a manipulative character who tries to fool everyone. When he is subsequently fooled by someone stronger than him, he admits defeat by giving his daughter's hand in marriage to Bel Ami.

FEMALE CHARACTERS

Clotilde de Marelle

Duroy's first romantic and worldly victory, Clotilde de Marelle remains an ongoing support for him and the object of recurrent desire, even after Bel Ami's two marriages. This attachment that he keeps is undoubtedly linked to the fact that he did not have to seduce her for a socio-professional promotion.

Madeleine Forestier-Duroy

An attractive yet mysterious woman, Madeleine reveals nothing of her origins. Her composure and calmness are admirable, allowing her to face any kind of situation, even the most embarrassing. She leads her life as a businessman and only gives herself to a man if she is certain there are benefits to be gained in return: Forestier serves as a mouthpiece; Duroy resumes the role of the latter; Comte de Vaudrec ensures her a dowry and financial affluence; Laroche-Mathieu fills her salon with the social world. She is the very image of a modern woman who leads her own life, uses men to her advantage, often despite themselves and places freedom above any other value, especially above fidelity.

Madame Walter

Early in the novel, Madame Walter embodies the honest woman who is faithful to her husband, even if she doesn't love him. She has never known a love story. When Bel Ami enters her life, she questions all of her principles and agrees to succumb to him. But this gift requires effort as she remains torn between reason and passion.

Naïve in love, she nevertheless knows how to handle difficult affairs and has a good understanding of political and economic situations. Bel Ami also benefits from her intelligence.

When Bel Ami neglects her, she is wounded, adopts a pious attitude and repents. On the announcement of Duroy's remarriage, she suffers from the situation she is in. She almost comes to hate her own daughter for being chosen by her former lover. Her passion, which becomes incontrollable, turns into dementia.

Suzanne Walter

Suzanne, like her mother, is a naïve woman. She was brought up in a bourgeois environment which did not prepare her for the pitfalls of real life. Her dreams and ideas of love blind her and prevent her from reacting with discernment. Her heart is pristine and pure. She allows herself to be carried away by the promises of Bel Ami and acts with all the stubbornness of her youth.

In the eyes of Bel Ami, even though he finds certain charms to her, she represents only one thing. She is his ticket to a life envied by all.

ANALYSIS

Women do not play the role of perfect wives or idealized mistresses in this story, as is the case in the majority of novels from previous generations. They have a new and specific role: to enable social progress. Following this principle, Bel Ami does not have the time to love a woman as each relationship allows him to take a step forward and move on to the next stage – and the next woman.

However, although the women allow for success, this does not stop them from committing adultery themselves. They cheat on their husbands with or without their consent. This rule applies to all of the women: Clotilde and Madeleine, who are more liberated, but also, and in particular, Madame Walter, no matter how bourgeois and Christian she may be. Love is not possible between human beings since they live side by side while lying and ignoring each other completely.

Similarly, marriage is not seen as an act of love. It is, in the words of Madeleine, a "partnership" which above all demands complete freedom within the marriage relationship (Part One, Chapter 8). Also, at the end of the novel, marriage, for Duroy, is a personal consecration.

In short, women, to Bel Ami, are one of two types: they are either free educators who allow him to drive in and establish himself in the world, such as Madeleine and Clotilde; or, they are just stepping stones towards social success, such as the Walter women.

Bel Ami shows that newspapers are the first force of any regime, whatever it may be. In this novel, the newspaper is *La Vie Française*.

A newspaper first owes its reputation to the external image it projects. This is to impose upon the eyes of others, and that is what the newspaper does, especially when we are shown the gathering of the editors engaging in a cup and ball game. Image is also the reason why Walter forces Duroy to accept the duel with the man who openly criticized him.

The center of the newspaper is the *Echoes*: "It is through them that rumors are set afloat and the public and the financial markets influenced" (Part One, Chapter 6). Duroy, head of the *Echoes*, becomes the one who creates and destroys everything, and the one who guesses what will please the public. Here, information is nothing but manipulation and the success of the newspaper ultimately depends on the expertise of its columnist.

Finally, we must recognize that, in this universe, the press is all-powerful when it becomes an accomplice to politics. Through the press, Duroy manages to build the character of Laroche-Mathieu, the future minister and ideal person for the job, but he also manages to quickly demolish it, unscrupulously and in only a few sharp lines. The press and money thus dominate politics and govern the entire Third Republic.

A NOVEL BETWEEN REALISM AND NATURALISM

On its publication, the novel was identified as a realist novel:

- Indeed, Maupassant describes a real universe: money, politics and journalism were realist themes already addressed by Balzac (a pioneer of realism in literature, 1799-1850);
- The characters, embodying passions and vices, are also realistic thanks to the punctilious descriptions of the author and their different natures;
- The novel is set in a context which is clearly linked to a real time period: the Third Republic. The "Tunisian affair", that shook the French financial world in 1881, also resurfaces line for line in the "Morocco affair".

Good to know: Realism

Realism is a literary movement that emerged in the mid-nineteenth century. It is characterized by the desire to imitate reality: for writers, the aim is to be as objective as possible. Therefore, they no longer seek to idealize what they describe, but to describe reality exactly as it is.

Some have even claimed that *Bel Ami* is a naturalist novel. It is true that all of the small details that fix the portrait of the characters, the swarm of people in a world of profit and, above all, the choice of a specific place as a point of study are all similarities to the novel *Money* by Zola (major figure of naturalism, 1840-1902). Maupassant talks of things that he knows from experience and which he can describe in minute detail. In this light, the novel really takes a naturalist perspective: Maupassant places his characters in a precise field of existence, that of money and the press, and observes their evolution in this field.

However, unlike Zola, Maupassant refuses to make his novel an overall scientific study. He selects certain social circles which he describes as a priority: the bourgeois, the nobles, the rich and the successful. The little people are completely excluded from his work. In addition, Maupassant's novel is led by plotting: the death of Forestier leaves a position open for Duroy to marry Madeleine, he does not marry her religiously, so that he can marry Suzanne afterwards. Everything is constructed to fit into the plot, not to study the possible reactions of a character in a given environment.

Good to know: Naturalism

Naturalism is an extension of realism. Naturalist novelists intend to show how man obeys a double determinism: he is firstly influenced by biological heredity, and secondly by the environment in which he lives. To do this, writers apply a scientific method to their works: after observing reality, they formulate a hypothesis and verify it through experimentation. They place a certain character in a precise story and follow the sequence of events that result from the double determinism described above. This approach, which aims to be scientific, should lead to a better understanding of man.

AUTOBIOGRAPHICAL ELEMENTS

Maupassant gives his hero some of his own traits, his mustache, his taste for women and his own anxieties. Both live similar experiences and follow a similar path. Yet, *Bel Ami* is and remains a work of fiction; it is not an autobiographical novel.

As we know, an autobiography is defined as "an introspective prose narrative that a real person writes about their own existence, which focuses on their personal life, particularly on the history of their personality (definition by P. Lejeune, 1975). In an autobiography, there is, therefore, a correspondence between the author, the narrator and the main character.

Here, one can find the beginnings of an idea later developed by Proust (French writer, 1871-1922) in his novels: to describe a social environment and establish a curious similarity between the main character and the author. Proust denies having written autobiographical novels, using the thesis presenting the narrator or the main character as another "self" than the real author. One can easily imagine that Maupassant took the same approach as Proust in *Bel Ami*.

Elsewhere in *Bel Ami*, we find a strong presence of autotextuality. With Georges Duroy, Maupassant reuses the character of Captain Épivent, who appears in *Gil Blas*. It also includes the theme of jealous husbands and their dead friends (here, Forestier) which Maupassant had already introduced in a short story entitled *His Avenger*.

FURTHER REFLECTION

SOME QUESTIONS TO THINK ABOUT...

- Explain what makes this a coming-of-age story. Can Georges Duroy be considered a hero? Explain your answer.
- After the death of Forestier, why does Bel Ami no longer feel anything but repulsion towards his former friend?
- How is the press represented? In what way is this novel a satire of the press?
- How does Maupassant depict the bourgeois world of his time? Do you think he sought to publish a criticism of this world?
- Can this novel be considered noir fiction?
- In your opinion, is this novel more realist or naturalist?
- Do you think *Bel Ami* can be considered an autobiography?
- This novel has been the subject of numerous television adaptations. Why do you think the story translates so well to the screen?

We want to hear from you!
Leave a comment on your online library
and share your favourite books on social media!

FURTHER READING

REFERENCE EDITION

- De Maupassant, G. (Unknown) *Bel-Ami*. Lausanne: Éditions Rencontre.

REFERENCE STUDIES

- Botterel, C. and Delaisement, G. (1999) Bel-Ami *de Guy de Maupassant*. Paris: Hatier.

ADAPTATIONS

Bel Ami has been the subject of numerous cinema and television adaptations, including:

- *Bel Ami*. (2012) [Film]. Declan Donnellan and Nick Ormerod. Dirs. UK/Italy: Redwave Films.

Bright ≣Summaries.com

More guides to rediscover your love of literature

Animal Farm
BY GEORGE ORWELL

The Stranger
BY ALBERT CAMUS

Harry Potter and the Sorcerer's Stone
BY J.K. ROWLING

The Silence of the Sea
BY VERCORS

Antigone
BY JEAN ANOUILH

The Flowers of Evil
BY BAUDELAIRE

www.brightsummaries.com

©BrightSummaries.com, 2016. All rights reserved.

www.brightsummaries.com

Ebook EAN: 9782806270269

Paperback EAN: 9782806272775

Legal Deposit: D/2015/12603/574

Cover: © Primento

Digital conception by Primento, the digital partner of publishers.